ON SECOND THOUGHTS

BY

MICHAEL GORDON DICKSON

Cover photograph is of the statue of the ram in Moffat High
Street, symbol of Moffat, Dumfries and Galloway.

DEDICATION

FOR MARY

ACKNOWLEDGMENTS

Once again I offer a massive "thank you" to my dear friend, Janet, proof reader, mentor, advisor, guru, and bookbinder all in one person.

ABOUT THE AUTHOR

Michael was born in Scotland's capital, Edinburgh, the only son of a family of theatrical producers. Charles and Ilona Ross, his grandfather and his mother, devised and produced the variety revue "Half-Past-Eight", which played to permanently full houses through the late forties and fifties in all of Scotland's top theatres. Subsequently, the author's early years were spent surrounded by show business legends as his "Uncles and Aunts". He chose not to follow his family into the theatre and also turned down professional status when singing in his teenage years for Edinburgh rock band, "The Kommodores"

Later in life, he purchased a public bar in partnership in Easter Road, Edinburgh, in close proximity to the stadium of his beloved Hibernian F.C.. Close friends would remark that it became the stage that he had always denied himself. He managed the bar for some twenty years.

Upon marrying Mary, they moved to the picturesque Scottish border town of Moffat where they raised their children, Lee, Sean and Holly. He has written music for amateur productions and church and is currently working on a book of his experiences of running a bar.

Also by this author, "Mountains and Molehills"

TABLE OF CONTENTS

ON SECOND THOUGHTS

I'm weighing up the situation
Considering each implication
This needs some consideration
Before I can decide.

Don't rush me into a decision
Which later, might invite derision,
This must be thought through with precision
Before my hands are tied.

I wish I could leave this behind
Conclusions are so hard to find
I wish I could make up my mind
About what I'm going to do.

I know that I must be incisive
I don't want to be divisive
But I'm not one to be decisive
And I've got to think this through.

Now my head is getting sore,
Please let me have a moment more
Before I can be sure
But I won't give up this fight.

I'm sorry for all this confusion
And it may be a delusion
But I can't reach a conclusion
About a choice that's right.

Forgive me all this hesitation
Concerning my prevarication
I've searched my brain for inspiration
And just come up with noughts.

But now, the waiter's cross I see......
I think......... That coffee's bad for me..............
So.......I'll just have a cup of tea!
But then again......
On second thoughts......

THIS MOMENT

Life is for today.
Yesterdays but memories,
Success or failure, entrenched within the past.
Remorse, the legacy of wayward footsteps,
Joy, the fleeting days that could not last.

And what is done is locked and sealed
By sands of time,
Reflections are the only gate to days gone by
Yet every backward page that's turned
Evokes a lesson
Through experience to the discerning eye.

And the future tells of nought,
Enshrouded in a mist
And tomorrows are uncertain in their number,
For when night shadows fall
May we be sure
That with the morning sun, we waken from our
slumber?

He who designs his course ahead,
Is less a wise man than a fool
For his plans may not be what the fates allow.
If present time is occupied with next achievement,
It comes to nothing with a sudden final bow.

For what we truly have
Is not to come or has gone by,
It is this moment, this hour and is this day
And should we fill each precious second
With the best that we can do,
We will have recognised
That life is for today.

CHURCH MOUSE

His antique candlestick
Fell off the grand piano,
He got down on his knees and held up several bits.
He shouted out "This can't be saved!"
And he ranted and he raved.
Where I was hiding, I was scared out of my wits.

He is obsessive about guarding
His Picasso
For it is worth a fortune, I once heard him say.
He has no faith in lucky charms,
He installed lasers and alarms
And has an armed guard to patrol it night and day.

Late at night, he will study
His computer
Concerning stocks and shares and gilts and bonds'
returns.
Sometimes then, he will weep
And I can't get to sleep
For all night long, he tosses and he turns.

Come early morning, he stands
At the bow window
And he will gaze expressionless
At distant hills
Then at breakfast, he sits grim, while it is brought

to him
And beside his plate, there are so many pills.

The end of breakfast, ends the time
He has alone
For meetings fill each working hour
That he has got....
Accountants and directors, estate agents and investors,
His gamekeeper and the captain of his yacht.

Then today, his stable manager arrived
And said he must confirm
The worst of all their fears.
Their champion tripped up and now was lamed for
the gold cup
Then all day long, I had my paws over my ears.

No more Camembert and no more
Danish blue.
No more cordon bleu to which
I have been treated.
No more deep pile carpets for my paws,
No more five star mouse hole, centrally heated.

For tonight I'll gather up
My few possessions
And to the chapel on the hill
I will move house.
The crumbs the gentle padre leaves, will barely cover
all my needs
But I will live in peace

As poor as a church mouse.

WHO AM I?

If I hear your cry of pain and close my ears
If I retain a heart of stone to see your tears
If I see you lying there and walk on by,
Who are you to me
And who am I?

If I refuse to share your burden on the way
If I turn my back when you are old and grey
If you seek the truth and I propound a lie,
Who are you to me
And who am I?

If I offer not my sight when you are blind
If I withhold a word of hope to troubled mind
If I am absent at your bedside as you die,
Who are you to me
And who am I?

If I do not hold my arm out when I see that you are
lame
And when you fall, pretend my eyes don't see,
If I do not quench your thirst when your lips
are parched and dry,
The one who is diminished
Will be me.

For no-one takes this walk of life alone
But in this vale of tears the seeds of love are sown
So you must be as dear to me as any other,
For you are my fellow man
I am your brother.

A SANDWICH AND A BLANKET.

I would not have asked for much.
I might have seen the morning light.
Just a sandwich and a blanket
May have got me through the night.

But the winter set in hard
Temperatures fell way below
The wind came from the north,
The biting cold
Came with the snow.

When life fails to bring success
And failure is your lot,
Life and death is finely balanced
Between the haves and the have-nots

But I never stooped to envy,
Lady luck can take and give.
Whatever she dispenses
Is the way that you must live.

And I always understood
If my outstretched hand was cursed

That I might have done likewise
If the roles had been reversed.

Yet when I laid my head on stone
And prayed for sanity to keep
The kindly face who'd pressed my palm
Was the angel of my sleep.

But my angels hurried past today
In driving wind and snow
To their homes with warmth and comfort.
They had somewhere to go.

And I would not have asked for much
For the will was lost to fight
But just a sandwich and a blanket
May have got me through the night.

THE BIRTHDAY PRESENT

I'd never told my wife a lie before
Until I told her I was out of cigarettes,
She looked at me in doubt
When I said I was going out
But this was all about her love of pets.

For tomorrow, we would celebrate her birthday
And passing the pet shop, I had seen an ad there
For the cutest little kitten
And I knew she would be smitten
When in the morning, I presented it to her.

I rushed to the address that I'd been given
And was amazed to find who opened up the door,
For Christine was her name
And she was an old flame
And we laughed to find that we had met once more.

When she took me in to see the fluffy kitten,
I knew my darling wife would be over the moon
But she said a man had viewed it
And for his daughter said he'd choose it

And he'd be back to pay her very soon.

I said, "A deal is never closed until it's paid for.
He who puts his cash down first, must be the boss."
I said "I'll tell you what I'll do,
I 'll leave fifty pounds with you
To compensate the daughter for her loss."

To my astonishment then she began to cry
As I picked up the kitten and put the cash down.
She said "I have to let you know
That I should not have let you go,
To have left a man like you, I was a clown."

And then amazingly, she threw her arms around me
And whispered that losing me had been a sin.
She stroked my cheeks with fingertips
Then kissed me full upon the lips
In perfect timing as her husband wandered in.

When he hit me, it was a great deal harder
Than I ever thought I could be hit before
And the blood streamed on my clothes
From my mutilated nose
As I was thrown, clutching the kitten, through his door.

Then I weaved down the garden path only to meet

A tattooed gorilla with rage in his eyes
He said "Where're you going with that?
That's my daughter's cat!"
I tried to speak but he said "Don't give me your lies!"

Should I compare this man's punch with the husband's,
Then the gorilla was the winner, there's no doubt
And the last thing I did see
Was the kitten flee
Just before I comprehensively blacked out.

When I came to, I crawled out to the pavement
And with my mobile phone, dialled nine-nine-nine.
The operator said "Okay,
An ambulance is on it's way
Retain consciousness if you can, for a short time."

Very soon a passing dog lifted it's leg
And began to urinate upon my suit,
Into the road, I rolled away
To escape the urine spray
Just as the ambulance ran over my foot.

I awoke within a hospital bed
With a bandaged foot suspended in the air
Then a young doctor sauntered in
With distinct lack of friendly grin

And said I'd be here for a while in medical care.

For my foot had suffered fourteen broken bones,
I had lost seven teeth and what was more,
It would be at least a week
Until I could try to speak
For I had a broken nose and fractured jaw.

He said that they would feed me intravenously.
It would be too painful to eat or try to talk
And he said meantime,
I should try to speak in sign
And in the future, I might limp instead of walk.

Then my wife came in with icy eyes of stone
And I waved my hands to try to tell my story
But she said she had no uses
To decipher my excuses,
My wretched secrets were now self-explanatory.

For Christine's husband had phoned her to confirm
The affair that had been running it's course.
She knew now when I closed our door,
I was consorting with that whore
And tomorrow she was filing for divorce.

When she had gone, my father-in-law marched in

And laughed to see me lying on my back
He said my job within his firm,
As of this moment he'd confirm
That he was pleased to tell me that I had the sack.

And as he left, another man came in
Wearing an animal rescue uniform and hat.
He offered deepest sympathies
To see my injuries
But was delighted to inform me
That they had found my cat.

LULLABY

Sleep, dear precious child,
Drift into stardust.
Sing with angels, dance with teddy bears.
Soon you will sail away
Somewhere beyond the Milky Way
To the playground at the foot
Of heaven's stairs.

Your innocence of soul
Will be your password
To a symphony of stars in angel flight.
When your dreams have set you free,
Blow the moon a kiss for me
But remember to come back
At morning light.

For you are still a very small newcomer
And all around you there is so much
You must learn
And the world that you came from
Soon will fade and will be gone
But in your dreams for now,
You may return.

And I will be here in the years ahead
To guide you.
In this life, stormy seas will always lie in wait
Meantime I will sit a while
Until I see you smile,
Then I will know you are at play
At heaven's gate.

If I could, I'd fall asleep
And be there with you
But my innocence was lost in years gone by
Yet I thank the Lord above
That he sent me you to love.
Now close your eyes and you will hear
My lullaby.

THE ONLY TIME I THINK OF YOU

The early morning is the only time
I think of you
When I draw back the curtains and I see the rain
And with my coffee I might find
That you have crossed my mind
As I count the raindrops
On the window pane.

And when I look through the glass
Into the garden
And see the cornflowers on display
In brilliant hue,
I planted them at your behest
For blue flowers, you loved best
Maybe then, for just a moment
I might stop and think of you

And when the phone rings
Or the bell at my front door,
I make the same mistake I always do
For as soon as I reply
Hopes fade and seem to die
And I wonder then

Why I had thought of you.

But those are the only times
I ever think of you
Except perhaps when walking down the street.
I meet people for a chat
And we talk of this and that
But all the time I look for someone
I really want to meet.

And when I sit alone at night
And read a book,
Strange things happen
I'm unable to explain
For I may have read so far
But find I'm wondering how you are
Then I must turn the pages back
To read again.

And as I fall asleep at night, then
I might think of you
And you are holding me the way you used to do
Then I drift away
And dream of yesterday.
Apart from that,
I hardly ever think of you.

CATNAP

The Sabre-toothed tiger
As far as I can gather,
Was my great, great, great, great,
Great, great, great grandfather.

Then we evolved in all directions,
Feline genetics had a ball...
Lions, leopards, cheetahs…
But we were cute and we were small.

Then these human being people
For no reason or no rhyme
Began to breed quite readily.
They were in season all the time!

And our cousins did not like them
Not one little bit
And likewise felt the humans
But we kept out of it.

Then they made clearings in the forest
And built what they call homes
But we stayed fairly close
And picked the meat from thrown out bones.

Then one day, my famous ancestor,
A legendary cat,
Jumped into their clearing
And pounced upon a rat.

And as he killed the rat
And held it in his claws,
The human being people
Gave him loud applause.

And they threw him bits of meat
And gathered round to stroke his fur
Then they all laughed and smiled
When he began to purr.

And the jaguars and lynxes
Called him a disgraceful cat
But we all moved in with the humans,
Thinking "We'll have some of that."

Then we found people called Egyptians
Who only seemed to bother
About spending all their time
Piling stones one on another.

And they venerated us.

To them, each of us wore a halo.
The only life-form treated better
Was something called a Pharaoh.

So the partnership began
And has continued down the ages
Now we live inside their homes
And catch a mouse to earn our wages.

And we are part of all their culture
And even their religion.
They pray in a cathedral
And teach their children catechism.

They call their daughters Catherine.
They parade on a catwalk
And they will scold their daughters
If they engage in catty talk.

Their sons have catapults.
They sail in catamarans.
They read catalogues
And when they're sick, they have CATscans.

They have mountains called the Catskills.
They live in Catalonia
And although they spelled it wrong

They have a country called Qatar.

If something's wrong, it's catastrophic.
Christians in catacombs had their roots
And they have made a superhero
Of a cat called Puss in Boots.

They have catkins in their gardens.
They grow catnip beside their roses.
They have cat's eyes in their roads
And they have catarrh in their noses.

So they made a good decision
When they discarded their mousetrap.
Now they can go about their business
While we take a catnap.

VIA DOLOROSA

Via Dolorosa,
Two thousand years have passed us by
Since you felt his bleeding feet
And heard his tortured cry.
The drag of timber scored your surface.
Echoes within your walls were locked
Of the sound of those who wept
And the jeers of those who mocked.

Loud, brazen calls still haunt your doorways
Shopkeepers telling of their wares.
Even here, another shekel
Tells of the depth of man's affairs.
But thirty pieces of soiled silver
Once betrayed a loving friend
And here in Via Dolorosa
I am not inclined to spend.

And I walk slow in total silence,
Immune to human din.
Every step touches my heart
With what we did to him
And as I reach my final footstep

I stop to draw my breath
And I look up to the hill
Where they all thought he'd met his death.

Then I look back at all the bustle
In your steep, narrow incline
And feel the images you hold
And will retain for endless time.
And I know, Via Dolorosa
When worms are entwined in my bones,
His blood and truth will ever lie
Within your weeping cobblestones.

AS DREAMERS DO

His dream launched him on the journey of a lifetime
And he disdained a map and spurned a chart
But he remained at ease
Although he sailed on stormy seas
For he left the navigation to his heart.

And they called to him to say he was mistaken
And pointed out an easy course instead
But he who says it can't be done
He knew, could never be the one
To hold a trophy up above his head.

For there are many who will choose a mild surrender
And others lacking the conviction to achieve,
So when they told him he was wrong,
He let his will be strong
And clung to his dedication to believe.

When in his darkest night, he ran aground
And foundered
And his spirit dissipated heart and soul,
He only had to raise his eyes

For him to realise
On the horizon, shining bright,
Still stood his goal.

Then he found the strength that no-one knew he had
And took his dream back down from off the shelf
And sailed on straight and true
As such people always do
For a dreamer is not beaten
Lest he admit it to himself.

And who can tell us if he reached his rainbow's end
And had a flag of victory unfurled?
But one thing we do know
He went where we were scared to go
And it may be,
We need more dreamers in this world.

DIFFERENT IN MY DAY

They don't know that they're born.
They're spoiled in every way.
They have it far too easy.
It was different in my day.

It's cash for food and cash for drinks,
School photos and bus fares,
If we found a penny in the street
We were millionaires.

Designer fashion clothes
Are the only ones they choose,
In our day we were ecstatic
If we had a pair of shoes.

Without their TV's and computers
And their I pads, they are beat.
The only fun we had was
Kicking tin cans down the street.

For pets, they must have fluffy rabbits
Or an expensive puppy dog.
I had an earwig in a matchbox

Till I swapped it for a frog.

And what a fuss upon their birthdays!
Don't give me the pip!
If I was lucky on my birthday,
I got an extra chip.

All day I'd do the housework
Then I'd make the tea
Then I'd do the washing up
When I was only three.

They must be driven in the morning?
Don't take me for a fool.
We got up at half past five
And walked ten miles to school.

They're still at school at fifteen?
What a waste of time,
As soon as we were seven,
We worked down the mine.

Three square meals a day?
We had no chance of that.
The only time we ate well
Was when dad killed a rat.

They don't know that they're born.
They're spoiled in every way,
But I'll be sure to tell them
It was different in my day.

I'D RATHER HAVE AN ELEPHANT

I'd rather walk into a garden
Than a shopping mall
And hear a symphony instead of
Traffic din.
I'd rather have rainforests
Than hamburgers.
I'd rather have a tiger
Than it's skin.

I'd rather listen to a songbird
Than a jet plane.
I'd rather mellow to church bells
Than hear road drills.
I'd rather sit and watch a deer
Than spot a hunter.
Instead of windmills, I would rather
See my hills.

I'd rather listen to a fool
Than so-called wise men.
Instead of tenements,
I'd rather see the sun.
I'd rather smell a rose

44

Than breathe in
Oil fumes.
I'd rather hold a puppy
Than a gun.

I would rather be a dreamer
Than a cynic
Though most of what I wish for
Cannot be
But I'd rather hear a clap of thunder
Than a bomb
And I'd rather have an elephant
Than have it's ivory.

LET ME LINGER

Let me linger for a while
The morning sun still makes me smile
And the air I breathe
Grows sweeter every day.
Soon daffodils will be in bloom
And they will pick some for my room
And from my window
I can watch spring lambs at play.

Throughout the winter snow
My soul was set to go
I had no rhyme or reason to delay
But now the birds begin to sing
As they herald in the spring,
So for a short time,
Let me linger
If I may.

Then this failing heart of mine
Can sing with nature one last time
And imagine her new life
Involves me too.
To hear the buzzing of the bees

And see the blossom on the trees,
I can pretend I will be part
Of all I view.

And somehow, it will seem so right
For my soul to take it's flight
Amidst your promise
That all life You will renew
And I will be content
To know my life is spent
And I will bless the world I leave
And come to You.

THE HAGGIS HUNTING SEASON

Precious few facts are known
Outside my native Scotland
About our rare and celebrated beast,
But from Blairgowrie to Dunkeld
Wherever Burns night may be held,
A haggis must be piped
Unto the feast.

Yet we Scots are enigmatic
In our nature
And there are many secrets we withhold
And it cannot be denied
That in the haggis, we take pride
But seldom offer information
That we hold.

When I tell tourists the whole truth
About the haggis,
With the same question
They always do reply..
What can be the reason
That the haggis hunting season
Is restricted to the thirteenth of July?

To explain, I tell them more
About the haggis...
That it will only breed at altitude.
In April at the Cairngorms,
They cluster in their swarms
And they climb two thousand feet
To raise their brood.

But once their cubs are duly raised
In wind and snow,
The descent is their most perilous of plights
And it is not a good set-up.
Many fall and then
Don't get up
And this is one of Scotland's
Saddest sights.

Now the survivors will escape
Into the glens
But their problems are not gone
By a long way,
For their diet depletes numbers
Since they only eat cucumbers
And many fail to see
Another day.

And if you roam the hills, no haggis will you see
Since the few that do remain
Must run and hide
For the diet that they savour
Gives their meat a special flavour
And poachers lurk
Around the countryside.

Then the tourists nod their heads
And they agree
That they fully understand now they know why
There is more than one good reason
Why the haggis hunting season
Is restricted to the thirteenth of July.

THAT KIND OF PERSON

I look into her eyes
And all that I can see
Is incalculable devotion
Which she concentrates on me.

If I am happy, she is happy
And her countenance is beaming
But should I have to reprimand her
Her life is without meaning.

Some words are never spoken
Yet on which can be relied.
In her own way she has told me
Her lifelong place is at my side.

She will never let me down.
I will never be betrayed.
I am the centre of her universe,
Her love will never fade.

But when I look into the mirror,
I shake my head at what I see
And wonder at such dedication

To someone such as me.

And I give myself a lecture
One to one and man to man
To try to be the kind of person
My dog thinks that I am.

LET ME LIVE

Let me know joy
Let me know pain
Let me sing a song in driving rain
Let my tears bring life to sterile earth
Let my heart leap to hear a newborn cry again.

Let me have eyes
That see it all
Let me at the wedding feast, dance till I fall
Let me bow my head beside a loved one's grave
Let me kneel in penitence, let me stand tall.

Let me smile
Let me sigh
Let me find the strength to laugh instead of cry
Let me inhale the heady incense of a rose
Let me shake the hand of every passer by.

Let me laugh
Let me weep
Let me never take a vow I will not keep
Let me never cease to chase a rainbow
Let me follow every dream born of my sleep.

Let me be pauper

Let me be king

Let me dismiss whichever life may bring.

Let me be ready to walk through a storm alone

Let me awake each day to hear a songbird sing.

Let me take

Let me give

Let me learn to be betrayed and to forgive

Let me sink beneath the waves or let me fly.

Do not allow me to exist.

Let me live.

SUPERSTITION

He never left the house without
His four-leafed clover
And he made sure he had his rabbit's foot as well,
No matter what the Scottish weather,
He always wore lucky white heather
Beside the evil eye in his lapel.

He hung a horseshoe over
His front door
To make his home a place where bad luck could not go
But one day, standing in his doorway
It ended up quite sorely
When the horseshoe fell and broke his toe.

He spilled some salt as he ate
His evening meal
Then threw some across his shoulder, where he sat.
He nearly had a heart attack
From the loud scream at his back
For he had very nearly blinded the cat.

At breakfast he would read
His horoscope.

It was his gospel, sitting with his coffee cup.
The day it said "Don't take a chance
On investment of finance"
Was the day his numbers all came up.

One day, a black cat tried
To walk across his path
And being a superstitious man,
He forgot his highway code
And leapt into the road
Where he was run over by a van.

He stayed in bed on Friday
The thirteenth
And rang the boss to say on Monday he'd be back.
When his boss heard why he was off,
He spluttered and he coughed
And told him that he had just got the sack.

Then he had a conversation
With himself
And said "I simply can't go on like this,
For I have made it my life's mission
To be in thrall to superstition,
To turn my back on old wive's tales would bring me
bliss."

And when he walked out of his door,
He now felt free
To spurn the past and to enjoy the years ahead
But the end could not be sadder
For when he walked under a ladder
A half a ton of bricks fell on his head.

THE PARASITE

It permanently dwells within our shadow
And with it's parasitic tentacles, it waits.
It holds to it's primal design,
Watchful for a sign
Of a hint of weakness
Onto which it may entwine.

Then it will squat and fester in the dark, unseen
And begin to surreptitiously infect
But it's work is far from done
For it has only just begun
And it's toxicity must spread
Before it's challenge can be won

Should it proceed with antidotes rejected,
Kindness and compassion will be lost.
It will dispense with clemency,
Replace it with expediency
But the casting out of love
Will be it's greatest victory

Now the condition is malignant, left unchecked
Though the recipient may seem normal outwardly

But he is no longer whole
For the poison has control,
His only function is self serving
Now that he has lost his soul.

And then the victim will be capable of acts,
Horrendous, inhuman and obscene.
The parasite has run it's course
With it's infection in full force
And whatever he may do,
He will do without remorse.

And the parasite was hatched in darkest hell
And of all of life's diseases, is unmatched.
Ever since the world began
It has flourished where it can.
It is called evil.
And it's only host
Is man.

DAY OF THE UNDERDOG

He's inconsequential.
He is no-one.
He doesn't matter.
He's overlooked.
He is dismissed.
He is ignored.
While trophies bear the name
Of some who rise to fame,
Obscurity in life is his reward.

He is the little man,
The back room boy,
He is timid.
He's deferential,
Unassuming,
Knows his place.
The background is his home
Where he lives on his own
And in the mirror,
He sees a faceless face.

Yet life may hold one single precious moment,
Unforeseen

Unheralded
Unplanned
For such a man to say
"I cannot let this pass today"
And to himself he vows
To take his stand.

With trepidation
He steps into
The arena.
The yawning crowd
Are unaware that he is there
But his opponents take their stance
Without a second glance,
Then he bows his head
In silent prayer.

Then he is beaten.
He is mauled.
He is knocked down
And in his whole life, he has never
Known such pain
And the spectators take a rest
For they are losing interest,
But they are shocked to see him
Get back up again.

Now the crowd
Lean forward
In their seats
And wince with every blow
That he sustains.
This time, when he hits the ground,
There is silence all around.
Then a communal gasp
When he gets up again.

And this time,
Unrelenting,
He is savaged
Till he stands swaying,
Fully bloodied,
Black and blue.
And in the stillness all around
His voice is the only sound
When he calls out
"Is that the best that you can do?"

Then one man
Rises to his feet
And he applauds
And the whole stadium
Takes the self-same route.
And they cheer in admiration

With a standing ovation
And his opponents stand back
And they salute.

It seems
That he was someone
All the time...
With a bravery he withheld from display.
Sadly, conceptions are retired
Only when hearts may be inspired
To see the underdog
Lay claim to his day.

THE ANT'S PRAYER

With her climbing party, halfway up a cliff,
She took a moment's rest balanced on a ledge.
A safety rope swung in her face
And though she held on to her place
Her dislodged contact lens spun over the edge.

Now much hampered, she continued with her climb
But her vision was distorted and was blurred
And when she made it to the crest
She sat to take a well-earned rest
While she considered what had just occurred.

Then the girl was moved to offer up a prayer,
"Mysteriously you work to reach your ends
But not one drop of rain may fall
Without you see it all
And should you will it, might I find my contact lens?"

Then her friends assisted her down the side trail
Negotiating loose shale and narrow bends.
When they reached safety down below
Another party said "Hello".
Then one man asked, "Did someone lose a contact

lens?"

And laughingly they pointed at a tiny ant
And in wonder, all that they could do was stare
For the ant struggled with the weight
Of a contact lens held straight
But what they could not hear was the ant's prayer.

"I cannot know Lord, why this burden I must carry.
It is so heavy and it is a bitter pill
And I truly cannot see
Why you are asking this of me
But if it is your wish
Then carry it I will."

Inspired by a true story.

TRAVEL GUIDE

I have never travelled to America
But I used to have a friend in Santa Fe.
He said "I know you're not a rover
But why don't you come over
And learn about the good old USA?"

I said I'd never felt the need to travel.
I'd never cycled more than five miles on my bike.
I said I didn't need to go
For I knew all there was to know
About Americans and what the USA was like.

I said, "I know that you eat nothing but hamburgers
Washed down with coke or sometimes bourbon instead
And you all chew chewing gum
And you all have a gun
And you wear baseball caps turned backwards on your
head.

You play a game called football mostly with your hands
And everyone wears cowboy boots of different types.
Jeans are compulsory
And all that you may see

Wherever you may go, are stars and stripes.

I know that you all skate to work upon a skateboard
And at the weekends, drive pink Cadillacs a lot
And your nation's heart was torn
By Abraham Lincoln
When in a drive-in movie, he was shot.

In New Mexico you have the Alamo
Where your ancestors with the Aztecs did give battle
And on a sunny day,
Should it ever come your way
You might take a trip down to Seattle".

Triumphantly, the phone emitted total silence
Clearly, to hear all that I knew, he hadn't planned.
I said" Then tell me what you know
(who'd never left New Mexico)
All about where I live in Scotland".

He said "I know you wake up to the sound of bagpipes
And you all eat porridge washed down with whisky
Then you all go out together
Marching through the heather
To your employment in a distillery.

And you all wear kilts with nothing underneath them

And you all have red hair and beards in quite a range
And no-one will catch you hopping
For when you have been out shopping
You will sit for hours checking your change.

And you peer into all your lochs looking for monsters
And sing sad songs about your army's worst defeat
And you will gather all your neighbours
To watch you tossing cabers
And you apparently play football with your feet.

To relax, you will go out haggis hunting
And should you ever get a cool day, take a chance
To take a little hike
Cycling on your bike
When you might even cross the border into France.

Above your house, you will fly a tartan flag
Like all the other castles you can see
And William Wallace of your race
Wrote "Amazing Grace"
Just after he'd abolished slavery."

I doubt if I will speak to him again
For though I do not wish to be unkind,
He should go back to school
For the man clearly is a fool

Almost as bad as all the know-alls
Who say travel broadens the mind.

THE LISTENER

Walk with me a while
Be not alone,
I have ears to hear a troubled mind.
As we proceed we may encounter sunshine
And begin to see the storm clouds
Fall behind.

This vale of tears is not a place
To travel solo
And be buffeted by hail and wind and rain.
Of one thing we may be sure
Life will command us to endure
But fellow travellers can always
Share the pain

For I have also known the misery
Of heartache
I recognise that grief reflected in your eyes.
A trouble held inside
Is a poison maximized,
A trouble shared is healing
In disguise.

Fall into step with me
And bare your soul
And I will listen till you recall
How to smile.
Should you fall back into despair,
Remember I am there
So take my arm
And walk with me awhile.

THE TEDDY BEARS ARE GONE

The teddy bears are gone
But I remember every one
And how I tucked them in beside you both
Each night.
Once love and laughter filled the air
Now this empty room is bare
But when I close my eyes
I see a different sight.

I see toys strewn on the floor,
Angels wings hang on the door
And between the beds,
The book of nursery rhyme.
It looked so forlorn
For it was tattered, it was torn,
I'd read it to you for at least
A hundred times.

And we played " Can you see...
Some things that begins with "b,"
Followed by compulsory
"I Spy."
The big match was on TV.

But strangely,
It meant more to me
When "another story!"
Was the plaintive cry.

Christmas Eve I'd dread
When I couldn't get to bed
For every time, around your door I'd peep,
Then I would have to step back
With Santa's presents
In a sack
And wonder if you'd ever
Go to sleep.

Then at a.m. five forty-five
The whole house would come alive
With decibels that could not climb
Much higher
And breathlessly we would be told
Santa had been
As good as gold
And Rudolph ate the carrot
By the fire.

This empty room makes my heart sing
Of the joy that children bring
And the laughter and the fun

We had to share
And though those special days are gone
A father's memories live on
Of the precious years of teddy bears.

Then you grew both straight and tall.
That was my prayer
Above all
Now you have entered in the world
Of man's affairs.
Now I sit at home,
Hoping you give your dad a phone,
But how I miss the days
Of teddy bears.

BAKERS DOZEN

John, Joan and Ian are my children
And I'm glad to tell
They are all in employment
And all four are doing well.

They all live away now,
Financially what that has meant...
My wife and I have cut outlay in half
Reducing costs forty percent.

I am fifty-nine years old
But when I'm feeling low
I know I can retire at sixty-five
I've only got four years to go.

So with retirement getting closer,
We must take care of what we've got.
I have ten thousand, my wife has seven.
Nineteen thousand's not a lot.

Our house was worth two hundred thousand
But now is ten percent reduced,
So a loss of forty thousand

For downsizing is no use.

And some expenses can't be cut.
I drive to work nine miles each way.
The weekly fuel costs are expensive
At sixteen miles each day.

My wife and I are happy
But there's one challenge to be met.
My job as an accountant
Is apparently under threat.

CONTENTMENT

The human spirit yearns to reach
A state of happiness
Where blue skies are perpetually in place,
Where laughter echoes all around,
Enduring love is always found
And the sun will ever warm
The upturned face.

And this phantom quest persists
Throughout life's journey
And at times it may appear
The cause is won
But it will have no lasting basis
For happiness is an oasis
And desert sands will call you to walk on.

Happiness is both illusory
And fleeting
And having been achieved,
Can seldom be maintained
But with ambition redefined
Man can possess more peace of mind
For contentment is more easily attained.

And contentment is the realistic aim
Of he who has discernment
In his soul
For he knows that in this life,
Joy is twinned with strife
But in contentment,
He has achieved his goal.

So leave the door to what you hope for
Open wide
But count the blessings you are given
For today.
Be content and then,
Perhaps,
Now and again,
Happiness will chance to come your way.

THE RACE

As if from nowhere, the track is there before you
With the first sound that you hear, the starter's gun.
It is not given you to know
How far you have to go,
All you know for certain is.....
That you must run.

And your first steps are uncertain, weak and slow
Yet for all the other entrants it's the same
And one or two fall in the trap
Of not completing the first lap
But this event allows
No waiting game.

Now your breathing is adjusting to your efforts
And you begin to find an even pace
And your stride begins to lengthen
As your legs begin to strengthen
And your heart leaps to feel the wind
Upon your face.

You help a badly limping runner to the sidetrack
And lay him gently down, only to find

It far beyond your comprehension
That some jeer at your intervention....
But you are fast and they will not
Leave you behind.

As you run on, you find that keeping pace beside you
Is a girl with golden hair, face wreathed in smiles.
Her every smile is an embrace
And you reach out to touch her face
And together you race on
Ten thousand miles.

But then fences are beginning to appear
And hand in hand you leap over every one.
What had been a flat race
Has become a steeplechase
And it is getting so much harder
To go on.

Then on the bend, there comes a fence that is much
higher
And your heart sinks at the leap
That is to come
And as you clear the barrier,
Your hand is wrenched from her
And instantly you know
Her race is done.

Then you stop and you cry out and kneel beside her
And as you hold her, your tears fall on the track
Then seeds of apathy are sown
To journey on alone
But you know this race permits
No turning back.

And you continue, but the sun no longer shines
And your legs are growing weaker all the while
And now the thought begins to grow
Of how much further you can go
And you long for your golden girl
And miss her smile.

You know that somehow you still have the lead
But you pull up and let the field run past.
A runner has run his last mile
So you comfort him awhile,
No longer caring to be first
Or to be last.

Now all around you, you are seeing others fall
Who have been running with you all this time.
Then you fall but you arise
And fall again and realise
That finally you've reached
Your finish line.

You have but moments left to look back on the race
And ask yourself, "Did I run straight, did I run true.
Did I give it my best
Did I pass the test
Did I do everything
That I could do?"

There is only one judge of this event
And at the rostrum now, you see him stand
And as your eyes begin to dim,
He beckons you to him
And he holds a winners medal
In his hand.

SAD REFLECTIONS

I'd had it for a long, long time,
Since I was eight or nine
And it always used to be effective
But passing years were bound to tell
Since the days it functioned well
And no longer does it meet it's main objective.

In times gone by, it would beguile
When it used to make me smile
Then gradually the flaws began to show
And I am sad to say
That it malfunctioned every day
Until the thought occurred that it might have to go.

Then with a heavy sigh
I gave it one last try
And I polished it and cleaned where it was stained.
I tightened joints that had got slack
But when I put it back
I despaired to see the problem still remained.

With a sentimental frown
I sadly took it down

For it was crystal clear that it had had it's day.
Now the dilemma had been faced,
It would have to be replaced
And in my rubbish bin, I sent it on it's way.

Then I went to the local store
But I was shaken to the core
When the assistant showed me what he had.
For if the truth be told,
I think I might be getting old
For every mirror that he showed me looked as bad.

COME TOMORROW

Come tomorrow, I will climb the highest mountain.
One day soon, I will write a symphony
And music critics will all praise it
As the philharmonic plays it
And the orchestra will stand to honour me.

Come tomorrow, I will write my life story
About the people I have known and girls I've kissed
And the publishers will fight
To negotiate the right
To put it onto the best-sellers list.

Come tomorrow, I will list those I have wronged
Through negligence or gossip or through lies.
I will cast aside pretence
And try to make my recompense
And humbly, to their face, apologise.

Come tomorrow, I will empty all my savings
And have my bank manager baffled and beguiled
But he will not comprehend
The course that I intend…
That every pound I own will feed a starving child.

Come tomorrow, I will search for my life's meaning
And I will study until it is clear....
The Bible, the Koran,
All great religions known to man,
I will read until I know why I am here.

But come tomorrow, if I'm called to take my leave,
As the mourners slowly walk away,
They will look at one another
And each say to the other.....
"If only he'd been given one more day."

ON A PEDESTAL

She put him on a pedestal.
He fell.
Now the young girl sits and weeps
Beside the wishing well.
She drops a coin into the water
And makes a wish for a fresh start,
"Please send me someone special
Who can mend a broken heart."

But if the outcome is not to be the same
She must first learn that mother nature
Plays a clever mating game
And is devious at playing hearts for fools,
So to play the game to win
She must first know
The basic rules.

For nature, in the role to procreate,
Must present to her
The more than perfect mate,
A smile will stop her in her tracks
And the stars will shine above
And she is then blindfolded

In nature's web called love.

And she will take one glance
In his direction
And all that she will see
Is sheer perfection
And to her wildly beating heart
She will profess
That he has qualities
That he does not possess.

But if love is meant to last
Our whole life through,
We must learn to love each other's
Failings too
And if she bears this premise
From the start,
Only then may it be safe for her
To give away her heart.

Young girl, I wish you years
Of happiness ahead
Into the arms of a good man
May you be led
And when that happens
And you want this love to stay,
This time,

Put the pedestal away.

THE ANNUAL HERMIT NEW YEAR CONVENTION

As your president, let me call you to order
And declare the annual meeting has begun.
In opening today,
I am glad to say
Our membership has gathered to the tune
Of one.

We say a prayer in memory of Isaac Grindlay,
Known as "Hoppy" as he had a triple hernia.
They found his body in a crevice
On the north face of Ben Nevis
And the autopsy said he'd died
Of hypothermia.

Of course we still lament our dear friend, Hector.
We still feel that ill-health may have been a factor.
Perhaps he suffered from dementia
Which might explain his final venture
When he ran from his cave and jumped
Under a tractor.

The hermit year has had it's ups and had it's downs.
For sadly there were some fatalities.

Rolf's corpse was found by mountain guides
And there were seven suicides
And we think we have lost Bert
In the big freeze.

There are times, within my role, I must take action
But the basic hermit laws, I cannot waive
So I had to expel
Member eleven, Seth McTell
When he was seen with a woman
In his cave.

We have one forthcoming event for this New Year
Which is the hermit health and safety inspection
So be sure your cave is clean
And your pet wildcat can't be seen
So that your hermit license
Doesn't face rejection.

If I may diverse for just a fleeting moment,
Member two, do I detect you slump and tire?
Come closer to the heat
Perhaps you need to eat
Please put one of my chestnuts
On the fire.

The anniversary occurs today of Hamish Whitehouse

Who composed the hermit slogan, now well known,
For the recluse federation,
Before he died of starvation
With the immortal words
"Leave me alone."

All that remains now is for me to say
That I urge you keep the maxims we hold dear…
Your cave is your home
And you will always be alone
And I wish you a lonely and impoverished New Year.

FAITH

I cannot know a guardian angel
Stands behind me.
I cannot know that part of me
Which is my soul.
I cannot know that my life has
A divine purpose.
I cannot know heaven is waiting
As my goal.

I cannot know my spirit has
Eternal life.
I cannot know that I never
Need despair.
I cannot know that I may always
Live in hope.
I cannot know that someone listens
To my prayer.

I cannot know that I am loved
Beyond my reason.
I cannot know that there are
Graces I receive.
I cannot see the face of God

With human eyes.

I cannot know.

But even so,

I can believe.

THE PRECIOUS FEW

They are the ones in life
To whom we are beholden
For the sweetest difference that they made
For there are not many who
Bestow their love on you
And for whom there is no debt
To be repaid.
The path of life is longer
For the lonely,
Our troubles and our joys
Were meant to share.
Of all the people you will know
Most will come and go,
Be true to those who stay
Because they care.
They are the ones who know your faults
And all your failings.
They are the rocks who stand beside you
Come what may.
They have seen you at your worst
But in your need,
They put you first
For somehow

They still love you anyway.
So put a value on their hearts
Above all others,
Cherish them with all that they are due.
Be thankful they have shown
In life, you did not walk alone
And know for certain
That they are
The precious few.

OTHER PEOPLE

If there's one thing I can't stand, it's other people
Asking blunt and probing questions as they do.
How I am is my affair,
Information I don't share
But when I meet them, they still ask me
How are you?

And who came up with the idea of neighbours?
Why are they there at all? The question begs,
Over the fence, they start to chat
Of boring this
And boring that,
Then ask to borrow half a dozen eggs.

Don't even talk to me of people in the workplace.
I drink my coffee quick in the canteen.
They ask, "Last night, what did you see?"
But I don't own a damned TV.
There's only other people
On a TV screen.

And why all of this talk about relationships?
Who said you needed children and a wife?

A woman telling you you're wrong
And brats screaming all day long
Is the surest way of ruining your life.

And then the family descend on you at Christmas.
A certainty to cause a major rift.
They drink your drink and must be fed
Then you can't get them off to bed
And they apparently expect to get a gift.

It there's one thing I can't stand, it's other people.
They are the cause of all life's misery
But I wear a broad grin,
It seems my luck is in
For it appears that other people
Can't stand me.

I HAVE A SON

I gaze upon you for the first time
Newly born
And with a tidal wave of love
My heart is torn
And suddenly I find
My entire world is redefined
And from this moment on,
Your life
Means more to me than mine.

And as your mother holds you close
I sit awhile
And all we do is look at you
And laugh and smile
And underneath your swaddling clothes
Again, we count ten tiny toes
And see you have your mother's eyes
And just perhaps your father's nose.

And I briefly put elation to one side
For a father must protect
And must provide
But looking at your baby face

That is a role
I will embrace,
A father's privilege
That will not be denied.

Then I hold your mother near,
Words cannot say
What my heart is telling her
Today
And I lean over the bed
And kiss your newborn head
And tell you I will love you
Come what may.

I will delight as years go by
To watch you grow,
I will impart to you
The little that I know
And I will pray to live as long
To see you
Handsome, tall and strong
And we will bear hug
Man to man
In macho show.

And as I step outside
Into the summer sun

My life has changed
But only just begun
And as I walk down the street
I will stop everyone I meet
For I need to tell the world
I have a son.

THE ARMS RACE

The good tribe first discovered flint
And sculpted primal knives,
Then if the bad tribe came to call,
They would pay with their lives.

Then the bad tribe ran afar
When of those knives they'd had their fill
But they came back with bows and arrows,
Now from a distance they could kill.

But the good tribe had good fortune,
They discovered iron ore
So they made spears and swords and armour
And scared the bad tribe to the core.

Then the bad tribe unveiled the secret,
They made swords and armour too
But they found how to make gunpowder.
The good tribe had to think this through.

Then there were muskets, guns and cannon,
For both tribes made the same
And they built boats and went to sea

And fought wars in their king's name.

Then they made bombs and learned to fly
So while one tribe lay in their beds
The other tribe could fly in darkness
And drop bombs upon their heads.

Then a small tribe called the dealers
Sold arms for battles, wars and riots
And they were millionaires
And they lived in peace and quiet.

Another small tribe called the scientists
Found each discovery they made
Was transformed into a weapon,
They shook their heads but were well paid.

Today both tribes are at a standstill.
And are checkmated more or less,
Both commandeer the earth's destruction
With a button they can press.

And testosterone and evil
Compound the folly and the sin
That the arms race still continues.
A race the human race can't win.

ROBIN

Robin, you know nothing of my life,
You are unaware that I have lost my wife
Or that I came here that I might be alone,
But you don't fly away,
It appears you want to stay,
Why are you reluctant to leave me
Sitting on my own?

With the passing hours, the stranger that it gets.
You watch me as I chain smoke cigarettes
And for one moment when I deeply sighed,
You didn't let that moment pass,
You stopped your worm search in the grass
And you looked at me
Head tilted to one side.

Your inquisition eye and your redbreast
Are seeming to put me to the test
For when you perched upon the bench near where I
sat,
You looked at me in such a way
As if you were trying to say
"You really mustn't feel as bad as that."

And I wondered at a life so simplified
And how you lived through the winter and survived
And how you resolutely followed nature's way
While humans strayed, betrayed and wept,
You fed, you mated and you slept
And sang a song of praise
For each new day.

Now shadows signify the coming of the night.
I must take my leave while you take flight
But allow that I may say before we do,
That it meant a lot to me
To have your company
And if I could,
I would fly away with you.

RAINCHECK BALL

They're trying to drag me to this big do
At the palace.
My fairy godmother has promised I can go
But Buttons showed me the guest list
And no-one awful has been missed.
I think it's going to be proper horror show.

That burglar Goldilocks
Has got a ticket
And that dimwit girl who lost all of her sheep
And what about that English rose
Who's spent a century comatose?
Why invite someone to a ball who's fast asleep?

They've asked the piper's son who is
A well known felon.
They've asked the idiots who think the king has clothes
And that boring man, Jack Horner
Will sit, pie in lap in the corner
And they've asked the lying puppet with that nose.

Would you believe they have invited
Georgie Porgie!

Everybody knows the rumours are all true.
Oh yes, he is tried and tested,
Every girl will be molested
And the big, bad wolf has been invited too!

At a ball, guests should be dancing
To fine music
With gentlemen asking ladies up to dance
But feet will not dare touch the ground
With three blind mice running around
And seven dwarfs and Thumbelina!...
There's no chance.

And the supper's curds and whey
And blackbird pie,
A "Song of sixpence" will be the only song.
I think I'd rather go to bed
With a migraine in my head
Than dance Ring-a-rosies all night long.

As for the prince, they seem to think
He's an Adonis.
They must have the libido of a log.
It's really got me beat
Why the girls swoon at his feet.
Hasn't anybody noticed he's a frog?

So I think I'll stay at home

And do the housework

Even though my hands have calluses and blisters

But if godmother has the grace

To make a miracle take place,

How about a plastic surgeon for my sisters?

TO TRUST ANOTHER

Human nature is both fickle
And unsteady
And it is ill-advised to build on shifting sand.
Taken on the whole
To trust another heart and soul
Is to risk a pathway on quicksand.

For it is there that broken hearts
Lie all around,
Weeping as their dreams turn into dust.
Of those who promise to be true,
The dependable are few
And only they may be the guardians of your trust.

The journey through this life
Teaches the lesson,
Be wary upon whom you may rely
So be regardful what you do
Should someone put their faith in you
Then on your shoulders
Responsibility will lie.

For no greater gift than trust

May be bestowed
But to accept it, enjoins you to be true
For with respect it may be given
But with love it may be driven
When another's eyes reveal
That they trust you.

Yet one day, will you walk away
In flight of fancy
When your ego tells you that you must
And leave an outstretched hand
Sinking back into quicksand
Or will you prove worthy of their trust?

FIREFLY

Firefly lead the way for me tonight.
Be my friend and let your lantern show
The path within my dreams that I must follow,
Firefly, take me where I have to go.

Guide me alongside a rippling brook,
Take me through the tangled briars and trees
Where the canopy shuts out the starlight
And softly rustles in the midnight breeze.

And then I find I do not walk alone
For rabbit tails are bobbing up ahead,
Badgers and a fox keep pace behind me
And a silver dove alights upon my head.

Now the animals are walking side by side
And forest birds are flying up above
But no creature shows another any fear
For this journey is a pilgrimage of love.

Then all at once a grassy clearing is ahead
And the animals move in and sit and wait.
Somehow I know that I may not go in to join them,

That to stand within the darkness is my fate.

Then as a shaft of moonlight falls upon the clearing,
A chatter of approval fills the air
And she appears in incandescent luminescence
With a moonbeam painting highlights in her hair.

And bluebirds come to sit upon her shoulders
While the animals all gather round her feet
And I envy all the creatures being with her
As I look on from my shadowy retreat.

And she talks to them and whispers gentle words
And strokes their feathers and their fur to their delight
And my heart is being torn as it is lifted
As the scene bestows its beauty on my sight

For the moment I beheld her glowing figure
Was the moment that my soul told me I knew
Yet when she turns her head to face in my direction
My heart still leaps to see that it is you.

Then my firefly's lantern fades and dies
And without him, I am banished from this place
But as my eyelids lift to reawaken
The feather of a dove lies on my pillowcase.

LOOK WITHIN

Betwixt the cradle and the grave
There lies a pathway,
At times it may be smooth and may be straight
But every foot that walks this road
Will be subject to overload
When encountering the fickle winds of fate.

Then the traveller's steps will falter
And grow weary
Until he finds that he is stranded and downcast
So he will not journey on
With his resolution gone
And will stand and stare at others walking past.

The fortunate will have a hand
Outstretched towards them
And willing arms to lift the burden from their back.
With such support then they will gain
New horizons to attain
But there will be those immobile on life's track.

They are alone
They are bereft

They are forsaken

With no-one to offer comfort to their ears

But words that lie on dusty shelves

Speak of the strength within ourselves

To ignite the spirit and confront our fears.

For only you can say

"I shall.

I can.

I must…

I will travel on and not be left behind"

And the process will begin

When you look within

And you may be amazed at what you find.

SATANIC MYTH

He doesn't exist.
And that suits him well.
He's a legend, a fable in his mythical hell.
His invisible cloak keeps his quarry blind
In his quest to hunt down the souls of mankind.
Should he be revealed in Satanic splendour,
Man would run to the arms of a god warm and tender.
Disbelief is more fruitful than horror or fear
But if man listens closely
There's a voice in his ear…
" I can give you whatever you want in this life
Be it fame, be it fortune or your neighbour's wife.
There is no truth.
There is no wrong.
Live a life of indulgence with the hedonist throng."
And his box of temptations with red ribbon tied,
Holds the worms of delusion
That fester inside.
But he's a legend, a fable in his mythical hell.
He doesn't exist.
And that suits him so well.

A TUNNEL AT THE END OF HIS LIGHT

I took a shower this morning
And found a new mole on my shoulder,
Fat chance that it's benign!
What if it's melanoma?

I look out of the window
To see it's drizzling a mite
But the rain might set in hard.
What if there's flooding by tonight?

My lower back is aching,
Another curse that's sent to blight us.
It'll probably get worse.
What if it's arthritis?

Now there's a letter from the revenue!
I won't be opening that today.
What if it's a bill?
What if I can't pay?

My cat is acting strangely.
She's sleeping like the dead.
Maybe I should call the vet.

What if the vet just shakes his head?

My daughter hasn't phoned me
And that's extremely rare.
I expect she's had an accident.
What if she's in intensive care?

Then the hospital will phone me
To confirm my qualms
And since the vet can't drive through floods
The cat will die held in my arms.

Then I pick up the morning paper
For my head is getting sore
And read the world is fraught with conflict,
What if there's another war?

Then they'll call up my only son…
If only I could go instead….
One day the ministry will phone
To say he's missing, presumed dead.

By then, with my arthritis
I'm sure to be in a wheelchair
And thanks to the tax office
There'll be no money to spare.

And I'll be getting radiography
To treat my melanoma…..
Too sick to go and see my daughter
Who is lying in a coma.

Then I'll be grieving for my daughter
And weeping for the son I lost
In need of constant nursing
But with no cash to bear the cost.

There comes a time to be decisive.
To face what lies ahead.
Now I've made my mind up….
I'm going back to bed.

I ALREADY KNOW

You don't smile when I say something funny.
You just say you've heard that one before
And try as I might
I no longer do things right
And I don't hear you laughing any more.

You don't take my hand when we're out walking.
Our anniversary, for the first time,
You forgot
And with every passing day
You have less to say
And it seems to me that you go out a lot.

The bracelet that I bought you for your birthday…
I noticed that you hadn't worn it once
And when I gently asked you why
You gave me no reply,
An embarrassed smile was your response.

Now when I reach out to hold you in my arms,
It's a one-way ticket, No return.
And I have to let you go
Because I didn't know

That you had something cooking
That might burn.

Your eyes betray that there are things
You need to say to me
And when you do, your words will fall
Like Arctic snow
And you will say it makes no sense
To continue this pretence
But you don't have to tell me,
I already know.

WEB SITE

Exposed to winter weather,
It can be hard to stay alive
So I sneak into your dwelling
For in its warmth, I may survive.
I try to find a quiet hideaway
Where I can be alone.
The corners of your ceilings
Make for a good home.

But there's the female of your species,
Sanity has been denied her
For she becomes hysterical
If she sees a spider.
She says she finds us creepy.
She screams and makes a shocking fuss.
Has she got no idea
How humans look to us?

She hoovered up my cousin Sally
And how could anyone forget
The day she trapped my Uncle Spencer
And flushed him down the toilet?
For her, the only thing as bad
Is if she sees a mouse

And now I come back from a walk
To find she's vacuumed up my house.

So I need to build a new one,
I search for a safe place in vain
And then I find an ideal spot
Behind the living room curtain.
So I spin a brand new house
And after all my labours,
I settle down in peace,
Well hidden from my neighbours.

But soon she pulls the curtain back
And shrieks for her husband, John
And I roll up in a ball,
I fear my spinning days are done.
And I pray to the Great Arachnid
Somewhere up on high,
Please may I be spared
For I'm too young to die.

And as they reach out for the hoover,
Suddenly they pull up short
And say "Let's leave this one alone.......
Look at all the flies he's caught!"

GLIMPSE OF ETERNITY

Entrapped within the flesh of his dimensions,
The basic facts of life he must obey,
For man must eat that he survive
So must work to stay alive
And in this process, he may live
Just for today.

Unaware that he has infinite potential
Which stark reality blindfolds him not to see,
So much consumed with daily strife
To ask the meaning of his life
Or too occupied to sense what he could be.

And yet, the day may come when he will ask the
question
That man has asked a thousand times before,
"Can ignorance be bliss, or is there more
To life than this and am I capable of being something
more?"

And when he lays his weary head upon the pillow,
His mind will spin with problems of that day,
Yet in time they will subside

123

And he will drift and glide
Into a world where blessed rest
Can come his way.

Then slowly stealing through the dark
Appears a gateway
Which is only his to enter for short time
And in this realm of the unknown
His answer will be shown
For there is no mountain here
He cannot climb.

Then just before he is enfolded in black velvet,
As rules of consciousness
Are ceasing to apply,
For fleeting moments he is free
To glimpse eternity
And he can reach out to the stars
And he can fly.

MY TRIBE

My tribe will not be yellow,
Neither black nor white,
It will not be Catholic, Muslim, Methodist.
Neither Mormon or Hindu,
Sikh or Buddhist too,
It will respect the love of God or atheist.

It will not swear allegiance
To the Tongs or KGB.
Nor the Mafia or the Basque separatist.
Not to the UDA
Or the IRA
Will not be fascist or be communist.

It won't be loyal to British bulldog
Or to the Russian bear
Or the Spanish bull or Uncle Sam.
My tribe will not permit a state
To teach it's people how to hate,
Whether in the western world
Or in Islam.

It will not be affiliated

To a secret shake of hand
It will not take part in protest violently.
My tribe will not be racist
Or be sexist or be ageist.
My tribe will not kill people randomly.

My tribe will turn away
From the lies of yesterday
Spoken without shame at polling booth
Political party membership
Will then be a sinking ship
And we'll appoint a man who always speaks the truth

Then the multitude of tribes will be gone
And we will narrow down to where it all began
For Eve was our shared mother
And each man is our brother,
The only tribe with our allegiance then
Will be the tribe of man.

WHAT LIES AHEAD

To know what lies ahead,
To know what is to come
Is a gift that man has been denied,
He may look into the past
But in the present, he is cast
And his future is a place
Where outcomes hide.

Since he found himself to be,
With curiosity unbound,
He determined to unveil the mysteries
Of the world that lay around him
Where destiny had found him
And as time passed by
He solved them by degrees.

Now he knows what are the stars
And how deep are the seas
And his frontiers, he diminishes each day
But the gift he is denied
Is a thorn within his side
For he knows not what tomorrow
Brings his way.

And prophets have proclaimed,
Oracles have spoken
And astrologers decoded astral law
And soothsayers have foretold
Of what the future has to hold
But no-one is any wiser
Than before.

For if he knew what is to come
Much would be altered
And his world be forced to change in many things.
His free will would be negated
For he would then be motivated
By his predetermination
Of what tomorrow brings.

Then hope would have no value
And faith could be dismissed
For the truth of life would fill his heart instead.
Now he predicts and he may plan
But it remains denied to man
For him to recognise
What lies ahead.

SEX ADDICTION

"Darling, where have you been?
All night I've walked the floor.
It was such a relief
To hear your key in the door.

You look so tired and so dishevelled,
In fact you look half dead
You smell of perfume, shirt stained with lipstick,
Your explanation now I dread."

"My dear, it couldn't be much worse,
Just when I thought I had it beat,
This wretched illness came back to haunt me
And swept me off my feet."

"Oh no! I feared you might say that
When you have fought it to the max.
Take your time to tell me.
Sit down, try to relax."

"We had a long day at the office
So when we got into my car,
Denise, my secretary and I

Stopped off at Valentino's bar.

We had one or two drinks
Then I began to wonder why
She suddenly looked so attractive
As her skirt rode up quite high.

I realised then to my horror
That I was having an attack
And there was nothing I could do
As all my symptoms flooded back.

Denise was so sympathetic.
She was so caring for my plight.
She said she'd take me home with her
And help me make it through the night.

And she stayed up the whole night through
Until the crack of dawn,
Doing all that she could do
Until my symptoms were all gone."

"My darling, you've been through the mill.
You've really had it rough.
To live with such a malady
Must be really tough.

Put on your slippers, I'll make your breakfast

Then I must not be mindless

To phone and thank Denise

For her compassion and her kindness."

WHEN I AM GONE

When I am gone
Then it must be you shall not see me
And my spoken word you will not hear
But it may be from time to time
That you think of me
And in such poignant moments,
Shed a tear.

Then from across Elysian Fields
That are eternal,
I will come from wherever I may be
And you will find that you are given
Consolation
If you close your eyes and smile
And think of me.

Feel it.
Touch it.
Sense it.
Know that
Your heart ever is enshrined,
When I was called, I did not take it with me.
For you, I left my love behind.

THE OTHER CHEEK

If a slur invokes an insult and a blow invites a blow
And a betrayal burns a bridge that will not mend,
And threats are duplicated
And slander reciprocated
Then a malaise is born that knows not where to end.

Retaliation is the enemy of love.
Vengeance is the carrier of hate.
Forbearance will retire
When anger lights a fire
And whilst man exacts revenge,
Heaven can wait.

For what begins as a slight from one to one,
Will then evolve a toxic life all of it's own,
Vendettas will begin
As it draws others in
And the seeds of animosity are sown.

Testosterone is in the recipe of man
That he may toil, he may be strong and stand his
 ground,
But strength is so much more

Than biceps and a jutting jaw
For in his soul, there is a power to be found.

And if one man draws on that power from within,
He will not offer a clenched fist to prove his worth,
And should he be disdained,
He may recall what is ordained,
It is the meek who shall inherit this earth.

And should this man stand in a row of ten men
And find himself standing in third place,
The second's struck by number one
And is told to pass it on
And number two strikes number three across the face.

But this man turns to face his assailant
And says, "I forgive you for what you have done."
Then seven men are unaware
That there was hatred in the air
For this man refused to pass it on.

The chain of anger will then be dissipated
When opportunity to extend it had been spurned,
For the malaise cannot live
With one who's ready to forgive
And who ends it when the other cheek is turned.

OLD SOLDIER

He sits daily in the park
Whether dry or whether wet
And I sit with him awhile
And we share a cigarette.

He sometimes wears his para's beret,
Holds up his head and juts his chin
And the march of time rolls back
To when no one would mess with him.

But now the years have taken toll.
The fight with cancer lingers on.
The whisky keeps him going
Since he lost his son.

And I know he wakes up shouting
In the middle of the night
For there are snipers in the bushes
And he's ready for the fight.

The echo of the battlefields
Are his stipend to endure
From when he walked inside the gates of hell

And took a guided tour.

And he can tell of stories
That can curl the hair
And he will curse and then apologise
In case somebody heard him swear.

And if he has drunk too much whisky
Which he is inclined to
He will keep asking God's forgiveness
For the things he had to do.

But still he loves to laugh
And I can chase away his frown
When I tell him when he goes
The coffin lid must be nailed down.

And as I leave, he's talking to the birds
And children passing by
And it's good to see the smile
In his sad and rheumy eye.

May God bless you, old soldier
For the price you had to pay
So I might have my freedom
To live in peace today.

R.I.P. Rennie Brownlie

FORTUNE TELLER

"Fortune teller, I've come back.
Please add the cost to my account,
My consultations have been frequent,
I must have run up some amount".

"Do not worry Mr. Pratt,
That is of no concern,
I know a glimpse into the future
Is what you truly yearn.

Please take a seat now Mr. Pratt,
Let us go with the flow.
I will consult my crystal ball
And we will turn the lights down low.

I see a financial building...
A man is running down the stairs...
He is shouting and he's weeping.
He is holding stocks and shares.

I see a woman called Amanda,
That name could be wrong of course....
I think she's in a lawyer's office

And she's filing for divorce.

Now I can see a doctor.......
A man is standing by a bed..
He's looking at an x-ray
As the doctor shakes his head.

I see ....what looks like Chesney Bridge.
A man is standing on a ledge.....
Now he's moving forward....
Now he's standing on the edge.

My crystal ball is fading
And there is nothing more.....
Some insights can be vague.
Of what we see, we can't be sure.

Readings can be misleading
And this one was average
Although your wife is called Amanda
And you live next to Chesney Bridge.

So do not worry Mr. Pratt.
Some things are not ours to know,
But if you wouldn't mind
Please pay your bill before you go."

IN YOUR IMAGE

When I was small, I climbed into my neighbour's garden
And I picked an apple from his apple tree
But as I climbed back down
A shadow fell upon the ground
And I found my neighbour there confronting me.

And he said to me "You are a wicked child"
As I put the apple in his outstretched palm
Then I tried to get away
But he stood in my way
And what he said next, filled me with alarm.

He said "I will be coming round to see your father
Then we will see how he deals with his thieving child.
Your father is a righteous man
And you should hide while you can
For he will be enraged to hear what you have done."

Then I ran home and I hid inside my room
Dreading how my father would react.
To have my father proud of me
Is how I longed for it to be
And with my head bowed down, I went to where he sat.

I told him of the bad thing I had done
But to look into his eyes, I did not dare.
I waited for the reprimand
As he lifted up his hand
And he reached out....to run his fingers through my
hair.

He said "I gave you life and in you, see my image
And I am proud to have a son who bears my name
And with the tears I look upon,
I see regret for what you've done
And what you took, you have returned from whence it
came."

I saw wisdom and so much love in his eyes
And all my doubts and fears, I cast aside.
I knew as long as I might live,
My loving father would forgive
And then he held his arms out open wide.

THE FIRST STONE

As we approach the stoning ground
There is much honour to be found
Dispensing retribution for immoral deeds.
Underneath the burning sun
Justice must be done
According to the holy book we read.

This woman's body could be bought
Until the day that she was caught,
The outrage of the crowd is fitting and is just.
Beyond contempt now she must be
Found in adultery
And it is only right that pay the price, she must.

Now she kneels weeping in the sand
Where there are many stones to hand
And expressions of disgust and rage surround her.
Her cries for mercy no-one hears
Her penitence falls on deaf ears
As we gather in a loose circle around her

Then they all look to me
For as their high priest, I must be

The one whose sacred duty it is to begin
To repay her decadence
With the appropriate vengeance
When she will earn the wages of her sin.

Accusers cannot be denied
Their claims are justified
For indeed this is a woman I have known
Who with my money, once was led
To join me in my bed
And I bend down to reach for the first stone.

YOUR BOUQUET

On my way I stopped and visited the florist
And chose your favourite flowers for the bouquet,
Lilac and gardenia,
Red roses and camellia,
I had them gift-wrapped and I went upon my way.

And as I walked, my heart was filled with precious
moments,
I felt no rain and heard no traffic din
For I was thinking how your eyes
Would show delight in the surprise
When unexpectedly, I suddenly walked in.

For the love that flowed from you held no attachments
Unconditionally given from the start
And my good fortune as I grew
Was to learn from you
How to follow and to listen to my heart.

And your gentle ways, your counsel and your wisdom
In my life's journey, evermore were there
And if I went off at half-tack

I was aware behind my back
There was someone who was offering a prayer.

Now I come to where you are and I go in
And I know by now where you will always be
And as tears form in my eyes,
I imagine your surprise
And your delight to see your visitor is me.

And I will stay and we will talk awhile
And your smile will chase my cares away
For there will never be another
Who can replace a mother
And on your graveside
I will lay down
Your bouquet.

DEAR JOAN (DEC.1941.)

Dear Joan, I'm sorry that I have to write this letter.
I'm sitting on the bridge we're building, It's half done.
I'm writing in the wind and rain
With my fingers stiff with pain
And I'm trying to shield the ink
So it won't run.

Every seven hours, we get ten minutes break.
To give us longer, the guards are too afraid
For if the kommandant gets mad
The beatings can be bad
And every night he checks the progress
We have made.

But the guards are not too bad most of the time
And occasionally they'll palm a cigarette
But you must not get caught,
The consequences will be fraught
For you will sleep out in the snow
Not in the shed.

The food we get to eat is just enough

To ensure we have sufficient energy
Although what we get on the plate
Is worse than second rate
And Jack and Colonel Smith
Have dysentery.

But I was thinking how you went through all my
savings
And how I tried so hard to keep us both together.
I had forgiven you for Bill
And then for Phil and even Jill
But every day brought only stormy weather.

So I write today to call the whole thing off
Although I promised that I always would be true
But it came as a surprise
For me to realise
I'm happier here
Than I ever was with you.

THE JONESES

I used to have some savings.
I used to have a happy wife
Till the Joneses moved in next door
And destroyed my peaceful life.

First they erected a gazebo.
The missus said that she liked that
So I had to build a summer house
Which cost ten thousand flat.

They put in decking and a greenhouse.
The missus said we must respond
So I laid crazy paving
And I had to dig a pond.

At Christmas time, their house and garden
Was one spectacular light show.
I had to buy eight packs of lights
And climb ladders in the snow.

Their kids had private education.
My missus fell into a mood.
We had to get a second mortgage

To send our Jimmy to St. Jude.

They took vacation in the Seychelles.
The missus went bananas.
We had to raid our savings
For a week in the Bahamas.

Now I can't take any more.
The nightmare's run it's course.
My house goes up for sale tomorrow.
They've only gone and bought a Porsche.

CHILD

Child, I sit and smile to watch you play.
You are slowly bringing meaning to my day,
A superhero or space pilot
Soon transforms into a pirate,
You are chasing all my cares and woes away.

And you are locked inside your world of make-believe,
Dull reality is not worth entertaining
Except you pause to ask one vital question
"Can we feed the ducks if it stops raining?"

Then you embrace some great adventure even more
And you deserve to win an Oscar
As you roll around the floor
And suddenly I am inspired to
Get down there beside you
But I am old and my back is too sore.

Now you look up and your voice is soft and low
And you say "I love you grandpa, don't you know?"
And my eyes are moist and tight
For my heart has taken flight
And I pray to be around to watch you grow.

But already child, there's so much to enjoy
In the persona of one bedraggled boy.
What matter noise and lack of neatness
When you shine innocence and sweetness
And make an old man's heart resound
With love and joy.

PERILS OF THE NIGHT

As the sun subsides,
Man turns out his light
Exchanging trials of the day
For the serenity of night.
But for others now begins
A gauntlet to be run
For they live in mortal danger
Until the morning sun.
The predators are stirring,
All is not what it seems
And now the battle for survival
Rages, while man dreams.
Be wary little field mouse,
You must take cover soon
For the shadow of an owl
Glides across the moon.
Doe rabbit, tell your kits
Not to make a sound,
The noise of sniffing
And of digging
Means the fox is above ground.
Hedgehog, stay on this side.
Do not try to cross the road.

There is a monster coming
With a heavy lorry load.
And mother thrush, be so afraid,
A weasel streaks across the lawn
And if he finds the nest
Your fledglings will be gone.
So the fight to live continues
In phantom hours of the dark,
In the fields and in the hedgerows,
In the gardens and the park.
But when morning light has broken
And danger fades away,
Man hears the sound of the dawn chorus
Giving thanks for a new day.
He rises and draws back the curtains
Gazing at the growing light
Oblivious and heedless
To the perils of the night.

I LOOKED BACK

I looked back
And saw the house where I was born
And the patch of grass
That grandma called the lawn
But howling winds were swirling by
Torrential rain fell from the sky.
The way that I remembered it,
The sun had always shone.

I looked back
And only loved ones could I see,
Each one had shared
A mile or two with me
And with no reward to seek,
Uplifted me when I was weak
And helped me try to be the man
That they imagined I could be.

I looked back
And saw my dreams of yesteryear
And all that lay behind that I held dear.
Would it be wrong for me to say
That I had come sufficient way

And ask if I might rest my soul
And end my journey here?

I looked back
And saw my mother standing there
With sunlight painting highlights
In her hair
And only every ounce of will at my command
Prevented me from reaching
For her hand
For I knew, in fleeting seconds
She'd be gone
And then I heard her softly say
"You must go on."

And I wondered at so many things
That are not mine to know......
Then I looked forward
For I still had some way to go.

WISDOM TOOTH

Albinos are the natives of Albania.
It was David Copperfield who asked for more,
And of course, I have heard of Tchaikovsky
I just can't remember what team he played for.

Now you ask if I have read the works of Shakespeare,
You think you've caught me out, but I have got you
there
For I have read " A Tale of Two Cities"
And on top of that, I've also read "Jane Eyre."

British convicts were deported to Austria.
Sigmund Freud directed and produced "Psycho."
To show neutrality, Pontius Pilate washed his hair.
The capital of Guatemala is Ohio.

Origami is the hobby of bird-watching.
Sir Walter Scott discovered the South Pole.
The mistress of a king is a courgette.
You catch melanoma by picking up a mole.

Handel crossed the Alps upon an elephant.
A euphemism's a horn in an orchestra.

A narcissist is a person who likes gardening.
The fear of Santa is called claustrophobia.

Now that I've passed your test on general knowledge,
I can see from your shocked expression
That you were stunned to hear all correct answers
To each and every one of all your questions.

But you can ask me anything you like
And I will answer at your beck and call,
I think that you forget that I am now eighteen
And at this age,
Should be aware,
I know it all.

GAUNTLET OF GRIEF

You will resent the fact that still
You hear your heartbeat.
You will see but will not see,
Care not to breathe
And from that moment, your future will lie dying
When you have joined the world
Of those who grieve.

Your mind unbidden, will fixate
On one thing only.
Grief will dim your eyes
And freeze your heart
And you will turn away in irritation
At well-meaning friends who speak
Of a fresh start.

But when the first act ends, there then
Must be an interval
And this intermission must precede
Act Two,
So lock your dressing room door
When curtains close.
How long the interval will last

Is up to you.

For grief contains ability
To linger
And to banish it, there is no known force.
The victim must submit unto it's torment
And learn endurance until
It runs it's course

Yet the day will come when you
Unlock that door
And for act two, rejoin the cast
And stand in line
And the curtains will re-open on your life
When you have yielded to the
Healing sands of time.

THE MASTER CRAFTSMAN

There are times, Lord when this world
Is all embracing.
My spirit like a windblown candle,
Flickers then
And voice of reason says to me
"Believe in only what you see
And be preoccupied with the affairs of men."

For I must work that I may eat
And may provide
And suffer trials and tribulations
On my way
And my perceptions are waylaid
And my horizons dim and fade
And a cold draught chills my spirit
Day by day.

Then this is all there is.
My world is no longer His
And the essence of my soul is parched and dry
And though I will journey on
Until my days are done
My final breath will draw the curtain

When I die.

Then I must step back from the mist
That clouds my vision
And release my soul to seek
That it may find
And feel the first warmth of elation
As I gaze on His creation
And leave the shopping malls
And tenements behind.

I see a rainbow in the sky,
A lark extols on high
And I inhale the scent of roses in the air.
Bees hum upon the breeze
And blossoms paint the trees
And my reeling senses genuflect in prayer

Then the mantle of His grace
Descends upon me
As I behold the Master Craftsman everywhere.
In all it's majesty,
It sings a hymn of love to me
And my heart leaps as I remember
You are there.

THE GREATEST SCOTSMAN

Here's to the man
Who first invented whisky,
Who created a beverage sublime,
Now I have filled it to the brim,
I raise my glass to him
For this man is a legend for all time.

Here's to the midwife
Who assisted at his birth
Who from the moment she first saw him
Would have known
He had the vision and the will to be
The builder of the first distillery
And give the world a drink
To call their own.

Here's to the mother of the man
Who gave us whisky
For she was the sacred woman
Who gave birth
And she should be beatified
For it simply cannot be denied
She bore the greatest man

Who's lived upon this earth

Here's to the father of the mother of this man
Who, one night met a girl
Who made him frisky
So then, he did take a wife
Who subsequently bore the life
Of the mother of the man
Who gave us whisky

And I drink to his grandfather and his mother
And his godparents, his uncle and his brother
And if he had a sister,
I'm sorry that I missed her.
I apologise to her
And any other

Now I must climb up on the table and must sing
A song of praise
And brook no intervention
For the world has to be told
About this liquid gold
And the sainted man
Who made this great invention.

But my audience is unappreciative
And I see the barman speaking

On the phone.

I'll drain the last drop from my glass,

All good things come to pass,

For he's calling me a cab

To take me home.

BAG OF GOLD

The last of his fingernails snapped
As he struggled to keep a firm hold,
The yawning abyss lay beneath him,
There in front of him, his bag of gold.

It was his life's accumulation
Gathered by lies and deceit,
Leaving others to weep in his footsteps
At his talent to hoax and to cheat.

Now his wealth tantalisingly lay there
Out of reach of his clawing grasp,
With each effort to clutch it, he cursed,
Choking heat from the pit made him gasp.

But greed motivates beyond normal
When avarice burns in the eyes
With sinews stretched out to the limit
He wept to take hold of his prize.

Then just as he cried tears of joy,
His heart stuttered in shock in mid-beat.

Something unspeakable, putrid and screeching
Was pulling him down by his feet.

Now he needed the strength of both hands
To prevent him from falling below
But he clung to the spoils of his life
And would not and could not let go.

And his pitiful long-drawn out scream
As he descended to hell
Bore testament to the life he had led
And to the distance he fell.

For he might have pulled back to safety
Should he have relinquished his hold,
Had he only placed on his soul
More value than a bag of gold.

BEING ME.

It isn't easy being me, for troubles know me
And they seek me out wherever I may be,
It seems they stand in line to test my resolution
And then it isn't easy being me.

It isn't easy being me when hopes and dreams
Are demolished long before they are set free
And I will weep to know that I must start again
Then it isn't easy being me.

It isn't easy being me when heartbreak strikes
And the blindfold of despair masks what I see
And I must find a reason to walk on
Then it isn't easy being me.

When a precious child is stricken with an illness
Or a heart that beat so true, ceases to be
And I must find the courage to be strong,
Then it isn't easy being me.

Then to rail against misfortune is so tempting
And to beg the fates to set me free
From the challenges and griefs that do beset me

Then it isn't easy being me.

Yet in this life, I know that I am not alone
In the trials and tribulations I go through
And if there's one thing I have learned
In little wisdom I have earned,
I can see it isn't easy being you.

WELCOME MAT

"Hello... before you enter,
May I ask you,
On the doormat, clean your shoes as best you can
For as you come through the doorway,
You will observe inside our hallway
A Persian rug which is a priceless Hamadan.

I will take you through into
Our second lounge
But may I ask you to sit here, not over there
For I am sure you cannot fail
To recognise they're Chippendale
But feel free to sit on any other chair.

Now Jonathan will bring you both
A sherry
But you will notice, not a sherry for the masses,
As the bouquet will make it plain,
It's from Jerez in southern Spain
But please be careful with the crystal glasses.

Should it be that you require
To use our restroom

The tasselled towels upon the rack are just for show.
Normal angora towels you'll see
Alongside the jacuzzi,
The designer towels are by Di Angelo.

Jonathan has just won
A promotion.
For his job application, they gave him five stars.
Now we may buy a villa
On the outskirts of Manila.....
My dear, please mind your elbow by that vase.

I can't believe the carriage clock
Is showing seven!
Too late to ask if you might stay to dine.
But maybe we can find a way
On a less busy day
To invite you over for a second time."

"Yes, of course, we must be
On our way.
Lord only knows where those eleven minutes went,
Appropriate words can not be proffered
For hospitality you offered
You must permit us to return the compliment.

But first, we have to clear

Our house of squatters
Before we can invite you for a drink.
Then we will have to wait
For the men to fumigate
And must remove the dead rat
From the kitchen sink.

MISTAKEN IDENTITY

There have been times I was mistaken
For a good man
When on occasion, I displayed the best of me.
It would be sad but true to say that I found comfort
In how others imagined me to be.

But impressions are merely
A veneer
Which may fail to reveal what lies within,
For they may be a mantle to a shining light
Or a cloak to a multitude of sins.

And if we define ourselves
As others see us,
Then we follow in the wake of a false star
For only in self cross-examination
May we authenticate the truth of who we are.

There, we will find the niches of
Our self delusion
And the many weaknesses we try to hide
Where the bonhomie and ostentatious kindness
Camouflage the selfish heart that lies inside.

Then to good works, is my inducement
Mere self seeking?
So that from so-called lesser men, I stand apart?
If so, then little I may do will carry worth
When my motivation comes not from my heart.

For if my actions are designed
To win approval
And to behold the praise within another's eyes,
Then I will have forfeited the value
And hypocrisy hide under my disguise.

So let my head be never turned
By commendation
For I alone know truly who I am.
Let any good thing I may do be masked in silence
And I not be mistaken then for a good man.

BE HAPPY

They said if he stopped smoking,
It would add years to his life,
So he gave it up against his better wishes
And they said that rabbit food
Would do him lots of good
So he turned his back on all his favourite dishes.

When they said he could live longer,
He paid heed to their advice
So when they said he must abstain from demon drink,
With a deep and heavy sigh
And a tear drop in his eye,
He poured his favourite whisky
Down the sink.

They said his body needed this
And his body needed that,
So he took vitamins and seaweed extract pills
And for his life to be extended,
Exercise was recommended
So he bought some running shoes
And ran up hills.

So he lived a long, long time
Till he was ninety-nine
And in a nursing home, he spent his final days
And for years, all of the while,
They never saw him smile
And the fees took all his life savings away.

Then just before he died,
Suddenly he cried,
"Bring me pen and paper, make it snappy!"
And when he'd gone, they found a note
And this is what he wrote,
"Have yourself a short life,
But be happy."

NEITHER DEAF NOR BLIND

Do you not glory at the world we see around us
Where a sunset's palette preludes starlit skies
And does your heart not sing to reach a mountain top
Where eternity unfolds before your eyes?

Can you look up at a towering cathedral
And not be stirred by what man can achieve
And may you gaze upon a loved one's smile
And not be moved by the warmth that you receive?

For around you lie the sights of all creation
Flowers, oceans, birds, blossoming trees.......
But sadly, I must ask you to forgive me......
For now I find that you are blind and cannot see.

Do you not thrill to hear a philharmonic symphony
Or catch the sound of blackbird's song on country path
And does it not mean so very much to you
That you were the first to hear your baby laugh?

And when you listen to the finest of all tenors
Sing a Puccini aria, have you no tears

And despite the passing years, can you still hear the
lullaby
That your mother sang to banish baby fears?

Do you not smile to hear the sound of children playing,
Or to hold a purring kitten to your ear.......
But sadly, I must ask you to forgive me.....
For now I find that you are deaf and cannot hear.

Do you not wince to hear the sound of bombs
exploding
Or to hear the strangled cries as people die?
Do you not see the fallen stones of the cathedral
Where with the dead, the blackbird and the kitten lie?

Do you not know for many, this is the last sunset?
Do you feel no grief to permeate your senses
When from a mountain top, you behold desolation
Where orphaned children lie weeping and defenceless?

Life can be preserved by words of wisdom
But such words, only peacemakers understand.
Do you ever count the cost of human life
Or do you merely count the money in your hand?

I must ask you not to ask me to forgive you
When you sell arms of war to spite humanity

For you were blessed not to be deaf or to be blind

Yet you choose

To neither hear nor see.

GOOD GRIEF, IT'S STUART BRUCE!

I thought my wife and I deserved a little treat
For recently she hadn't been too well
But we could just afford to take
A long weekend break
In peace and quiet at a five star hotel.

Linda was thrilled when we arrived but she looked
tired
And I could see our journey had taken it's toll.
I said, "The weight is off our backs,
Why don't you just relax
And while you have a rest, I'll take a stroll."

And in the elevator down, I smiled and whistled
For I was thinking "This is as good as it gets"
The doorman was so polite
As I stepped out into the night
And crossed the road to buy some cigarettes.

But as I made my way into the supermarket
A woman passed me then she spun about.
She gasped, "I'm having a breakdown

The papers said you were in town!
Good grief, it's Stuart Bruce!" And she passed out.

Then a wide-eyed girl stopped and started shaking
And she cried out, "This is beyond my wildest dreams!
Your greatest films....I've seen them all
I've got your picture on my wall."
Then in mid-sentence she descended into screams.

I shouted,"Look...I Am aware of slight resemblance
But I am told that that depends which way I turn
But please give me a break
For you are making a mistake.
I am an accountant from Blackburn."

But I might as well have saved my breath
With this unwanted fame that I had found
For now I was hemmed in
Like a sardine in a tin
And mobile phones were flashing all around.

I thought discretion was the better part of valour
 So I yelled "Ladies, could we call a truce.
All your autographs I'll sign
If you stand orderly in line."
But they just chanted "We love Stuart Bruce."

Then the situation suddenly got worse
As the supermarket tannoy blared away...
"We are proud to announce
The star of "Courage by the Ounce,"
Mr. Stuart Bruce is in our store today."

Then havoc turned to mayhem then to bedlam,
To reason with the growing crowd was of no use.
Suffocation I was fearing
While I was deafened to be hearing
The racket of "Good grief, it's Stuart Bruce!"

So I summoned all the courage that I had
And pushing free I ran like a bat out of hell,
A car screeched to a halt
And I did a somersault
But the doorman helped me into the hotel.

And he said "Sir, your leg is bleeding
And you have lipstick all over your cheeks."
I said "You'd best see to your job
For outside there's a screaming mob"
And he said "Good lord, I'd better call the police!"

Then shaking, I limped to the hotel bar
Which ironically was called "The Four-leafed Clover"

I asked the barmaid for a double
If it wasn't too much trouble
She said"Good grief, it's Stuart Bruce!"
And she keeled over.

So I hobbled round to the reception
And asked the lady there for my key to my door
But just as I had feared
She looked at me and disappeared
I stepped around her to pick my key off the floor.

Then a man in a smart suit hurried up to me
And said he was the hotel manager, Gerald Nash.
He said "We'll have to use deceit
To get you safely to your suite"
And handed me sunglasses and a false moustache.

Then he walked me incognito through the main hall
Where screaming girls were being ejected by the
police,
He said "The police are cordoning off the street
So I think we have this beat
And from now on we will ensure that you have peace."

And from the lift he got me safely to my floor
And said "Today for you, things got beyond a laugh

But as of now I hope your stay
Will be restful in every way
But for my daughter could I have your autograph?"

Then a smiling man was standing at my doorway
And he politely said "Excuse me sir,
People can't know what you've been through
But I can say, I think I do,
And you have certainly created quite a stir

So forgive me for imposing one more time.
Before you take some rest, I wondered whether
If you wouldn't mind,
You might be so kind
To let me take our photograph together?"

Then he held up his mobile phone to take a picture
Just as my wife came out of the bedroom.
She looked at him and she stopped dead
And in a strangled voice she said
"Good grief, it's Stuart Bruce!" And then she swooned.

WHEN LOVE HAS DIED

No arms to raise the fallen
No ears for grief to share
A crying child, a mother's tenderness denied.
No doormat saying welcome,
No door unlocked, unbarred,
All the world will weep
When love has died.

No concern to tend the sick
No remorse or clemency
Death certificates citing loneliness as cause.
No melody or rhyme,
Farewell to laughter.
Clowns will sigh for hearing
No applause.

Solicitude redundant,
Kindness become unspoken word,
Backs to be turned upon another's fate.
Sterile hearts that multiply
In stagnant waters.

Money changing hands
To procreate.

No husbands being faithful
No wives with fidelity
No graveside mourners come to say goodbye.
No coin to feed the beggar
No hand to lead the blind
And the earth will turn to salt
From all who cry.

And the sun will shine on no-one
And the stars withhold their light
For now the seeds of self destruction have been sown.
Each of us will be an island
In an empty, heartless sea,
Within a multitude, every man
Will stand alone.

From all other forms of life
We are unique
For our hearts can speak where words may be denied
But if those hearts speak only
To closed ears,
Our birthright is renounced
When love has died.

THE HARDEST WORD

The rising sun will bow and bid you Sayonara,
Stiff, British upper-lip, terse Cheerio.
On hearing click of German boot,
Auf Wiedersehen's the last salute
But however it is said,
The tears will flow.

Arrividerci will resound from hills of Rome,
So Long, the parting words from Uncle Sam,
Where the Old Testament is from,
You will be offered a Shalom
And Adieu will echo from
The Notre Dame.

But whichever way is chosen how to say it,
One word cannot reveal leave-parting loss.
Hasta la Vista does not tell
The pain of a farewell
No more than Au Revoir
Or Adios.

For if perchance, it is the final word that's spoken

To one who's loved with only silence in reply.
We will remember all our days
In so many different ways,
The hardest word we ever had to say
Was when we said Goodbye.